Dear Parents and Educators,

Welcome to Penguin Young Readers! As parents and educators, you know that each child develops at his or her own pace—in terms of speech, critical thinking, and, of course, reading. Penguin Young Readers recognizes this fact. As a result, each Penguin Young Readers book is assigned a traditional easy-to-read level (1–4) as well as a Guided Reading Level (A–P). Both of these systems will help you choose the right book for your child. Please refer to the back of each book for specific leveling information. Penguin Young Readers features esteemed authors and illustrators, stories about favorite characters, fascinating nonfiction, and more!

Civil War Battleship: The *Monitor*

LEVEL **4**

GUIDED READING LEVEL **N**

This book is perfect for a **Fluent Reader** who:
• can read the text quickly with minimal effort;
• has good comprehension skills;
• can self-correct (can recognize when something doesn't sound right); and
• can read aloud smoothly and with expression.

Here are some **activities** you can do during and after reading this book:
• Venn Diagram: Once the South decides to build the *Virginia*, an ironclad ship, the North races to build the *Monitor*, their ironclad ship. Think about how the two ships are alike and how they are different. On a separate sheet of paper, draw a Venn diagram—two circles that overlap. Label one circle *Virginia* and the other circle *Monitor*. Write the traits that are specific to each ship in the parts of the circles that don't touch. Write the traits they share in the space where the circles overlap.
• Research: The *Monitor* is a famous sunken ship. Do some research on other famous sunken ships. Choose one and write a paragraph describing it.

Remember, sharing the love of reading with a child is the best gift you can give!

—Bonnie Bader, EdM
  Penguin Young Readers program

*Penguin Young Readers are leveled by independent reviewers applying the standards developed by Irene Fountas and Gay Su Pinnell in *Matching Books to Readers: Using Leveled Books in Guided Reading*, Heinemann, 1999.

To my dad, Stan, a World War II soldier;
and Megan, for all her help. Thanks—GT

To Andrew and Peter—LD

Special thanks to Beverly Mcmillan

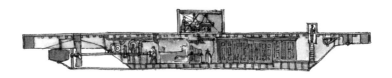

Penguin Young Readers
Published by the Penguin Group
Penguin Group (USA) Inc., 375 Hudson Street, New York, New York 10014, USA
Penguin Group (Canada), 90 Eglinton Avenue East, Suite 700, Toronto, Ontario M4P 2Y3, Canada
(a division of Pearson Penguin Canada Inc.)
Penguin Books Ltd, 80 Strand, London WC2R 0RL, England
Penguin Ireland, 25 St Stephen's Green, Dublin 2, Ireland (a division of Penguin Books Ltd)
Penguin Group (Australia), 707 Collins Street, Melbourne, Victoria 3008, Australia
(a division of Pearson Australia Group Pty Ltd)
Penguin Books India Pvt Ltd, 11 Community Centre, Panchsheel Park, New Delhi—110 017, India
Penguin Group (NZ), 67 Apollo Drive, Rosedale, Auckland 0632, New Zealand
(a division of Pearson New Zealand Ltd)
Penguin Books (South Africa), Rosebank Office Park, 181 Jan Smuts Avenue,
Parktown North 2193, South Africa
Penguin China, B7 Jiaming Center, 27 East Third Ring Road North,
Chaoyang District, Beijing 100020, China

Penguin Books Ltd, Registered Offices: 80 Strand, London WC2R 0RL, England

Text copyright © 2003 by Gare Thompson. Illustrations copyright © 2003 by Larry Day. All rights
reserved. First published in 2003 as The Monitor: The Iron Warship That Changed the World by
Grosset & Dunlap, an imprint of Penguin Group (USA) Inc. Published in 2013
by Penguin Young Readers, an imprint of Penguin Group (USA) Inc.,
345 Hudson Street, New York, New York 10014. Manufactured in China.

Library of Congress Control Number: 2003016953

ISBN 978-0-448-43245-8   10 9 8 7 6 5 4 3 2 1

ALWAYS LEARNING   PEARSON

PENGUIN YOUNG READERS

LEVEL 4
FLUENT READER

Civil War Battleship
The *Monitor*

by Gare Thompson
illustrated by Larry Day

Penguin Young Readers
An Imprint of Penguin Group (USA) Inc.

Chapter 1

Deep in the Atlantic Ocean, a mystery awaits. The mystery is the *Monitor*, an ironclad warship that sank on New Year's Eve, 1862. For over 100 years, the *Monitor* has rested in a silent grave. Sand buries part of the ship. Where sailors once worked, fish now swim. And no one in the world knows where the *Monitor* lies.

Then, in 1973, the silence of the deep is broken. Using old records and modern technology, scientists think they may have finally found the *Monitor*. The team searches an area called the "Graveyard of the Atlantic" because so many ships have sunk there.

Finding the *Monitor* among all of those other shipwrecks won't be easy. But the team is determined to try.

Why was it so important to find the *Monitor*? What makes this ship stand out among all the other wrecks in the area? What secrets are hidden within its iron hull?

The answers lie in the lost ship's history—and in the ship itself.

Chapter 2

It is December 1860, and the United States is about to break apart in a terrible civil war. People from the South want to start their own country. People from the North want the nation to stay together. This is only one issue that the North and the South argue about. Another one is slavery. Many people in the South have slaves that work on their plantations. Many people in the North want to end slavery. The two sides cannot agree. One by one, Southern states leave the United States to start a new nation, the Confederacy.

In 1861, the war begins.

President Abraham Lincoln wants the United States to stay together. And he

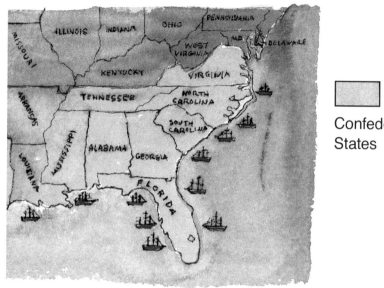

Confederate
States

wants the war to end soon. The North
believes it can win the war by blocking
Southern ports with fast wooden warships.
This *blockade* will keep supplies and
guns from reaching the South. Without
supplies, the North hopes, the South will
be forced to surrender.

The South knows that a blockade could
make them lose the war. But what can the
South do about all of the North's wooden
warships? Stephen Mallory is in charge

of the Confederate navy. He has heard of
a new kind of ship—the ironclad—that
is being built in Europe. These ships are
covered with iron. They are stronger and
more powerful than ships that are made
only of wood. And they are very hard to
damage. Mallory believes that an ironclad
ship could break through the blockade.

But the South doesn't have enough time,
money, or iron to build a whole ironclad
from scratch. Mallory figures out a way
to solve this problem. Instead of building
a new ship, the South will turn a wooden
warship into an ironclad. They cover a
captured Northern ship, the *Merrimac*, with
thick iron plates. It is slow, hard work. But
it will be worth it.

Northern spies hear about the South's
ironclad and report back to the United

States government. Gideon Welles, the man in charge of the Northern navy, knows that a Southern ironclad is bad news for the North. It could easily destroy many Northern ships. There is only one thing to do: The North must build its own ironclad. There isn't a moment to lose.

Many engineers design ironclads for the North, but only one ship will be built. One man, John Ericsson, has been dreaming of building an ironclad for over 25 years. Welles likes Ericsson's model the best. So does President Lincoln. For Ericsson, it is a dream come true! On October 25, 1861, the Navy begins building his ironclad, the *Monitor*, in New York.

When the South finds out about the North's plans, they resolve to finish their ironclad first. They rename the ship the

Virginia and work on it day and night. The North and South race to build their ironclads because of Hampton Roads, an important waterway for ships. If the South takes control of Hampton Roads, they would be able to break the blockade—and attack Washington, DC, the US capital. If the North takes control of Hampton Roads, they could

The *Merrimac's* original hull

Iron plates

keep the blockade strong. They could also attack Richmond, Virginia, the capital of the Confederacy.

Both sides are building ironclads, but their ships are very different. The *Virginia* is huge—275 feet long! It has eight large cannons, four on each side. Workers cover the top half of the wooden ship with three inches of iron. One of the scariest parts

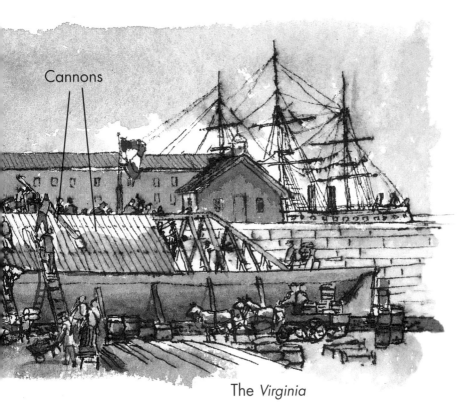

Cannons

The *Virginia*

of the ship is its large ram. Shaped like a giant arrow, it juts out from the *Virginia's* bow and is used to make huge holes in the sides of enemy ships. The ships then fill with water and sink.

While the *Virginia* is large, the *Monitor* is small. It is only 173 feet long. But the *Monitor* has some important advantages over the *Virginia*. Most of the ship is below the waterline. There, the crew will be safe from enemy gunfire. The *Monitor* also has a gun turret that turns

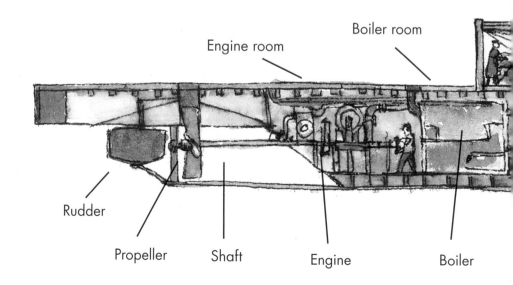

in a circle. Most ships, including the
Virginia, have cannons on their sides. The
ships have to turn to point their guns in a
different direction. But the *Monitor's* gun
turret turns while the ship stays in one
place. It can aim and shoot faster—and
hit moving ships!

Every day, Ericsson goes to the dockyard
where the *Monitor* is being built. The smell
of iron fills the air as men work around
the clock to finish the ironclad. To most
people, the low ship looks like it is about

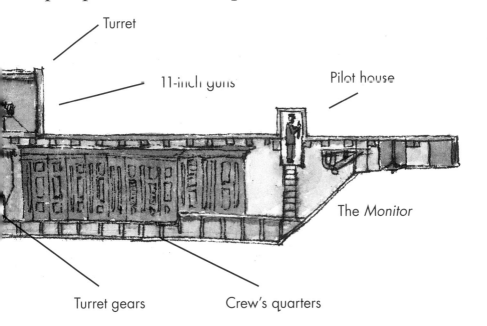

Turret

11-inch guns

Pilot house

The *Monitor*

Turret gears

Crew's quarters

to sink. The workers have doubts about the ironclad, too. The gun turret looks too big. The deck seems too small. Will this strange ship even float?

When the *Monitor* is finished, crowds gather on the docks to watch the ironclad launch on January 30, 1862. People have never seen anything like it. Some call it an "iron coffin" because they are sure it will sink. A rescue boat waits nearby—just in case. Slowly, the *Monitor* moves out of the harbor.

It doesn't sink. The crowd cheers!

When leaders in the South learn that the North's ironclad is on the move, they quickly launch the *Virginia*, even though it's not finished yet. It is worth the risk. Both sides are racing to Hampton Roads.

Who will get there first?

Chapter 3

Slowly, the *Monitor* makes its way to Hampton Roads. Captain John Worden leads 58 crewmen to protect the ships there. The first day and night at sea are calm. But the winter weather in the Atlantic Ocean is dangerous. It can change in an instant. And it does.

A fierce storm hits the *Monitor.* Its low deck fills with water. Waves crash over the pilothouse with such force that a man is knocked over. There is a leak in the gun turret. The workers who doubted Ericsson's design did not follow his orders. Now the crew is paying for this mistake. They are in great danger.

Then, things get worse.

The *Monitor* has a steam engine to

make it move. Funnels from the steam
engine let smoke out. Fans bring fresh air
in. But now waves pour down the funnels
and flood the engine room. The fans
stop. The engine shuts down. Poisonous
fumes fill the ship. The crewmen, gasping
for air, crawl to the deck. Huge waves
crash over them as they try to breathe.

Captain Worden orders the crew to
start bailing by pouring buckets of

seawater over the sides. At last, the storm dies down, and five long hours later, the *Monitor* is in calm seas. Sailors fix the engine and fans. Miraculously, the *Monitor* is on its way again. But the storm has cost them time.

While the *Monitor* struggles in the storm, the *Virginia* steams down the Elizabeth River toward Hampton Roads. Captain Franklin Buchanan is eager to test the ironclad in battle. On March 8, 1862, the *Virginia* arrives in Hampton Roads. There are two Northern ships there—the *Cumberland* and the *Congress*—that are important to the blockade. The *Virginia* plans to destroy them both.

Northern sailors on the ships see a plume of black smoke rising in the distance. It is the South's ironclad! They

have almost no time to get ready for this surprise attack. Soon the mighty *Virginia* is upon them.

The *Virginia's* first target is the *Cumberland*. The wooden ship splinters where one of the *Virginia's* cannonballs hits it. The *Cumberland* fires back, but its shots do not stop the *Virginia*. The *Virginia's* second shot kills many of the *Cumberland's* gun crew. The sailors of the *Cumberland* can do nothing to stop

the metal monster approaching them.

Then the *Virginia* smashes the *Cumberland* with its powerful ram, ripping a seven-foot hole in it. Seawater pours in, and the ship pitches over. The *Cumberland's* brave crew continues to fight, but the ship is doomed. Finally, the captain of the *Cumberland* orders his men to abandon ship—before they all drown.

The *Congress* has watched the fearsome attack on the *Cumberland*. The captain

of the *Congress* runs his ship aground
so that it is out of reach of the *Virginia's*
ram. But Captain Buchanan is
determined to destroy the *Congress*. He
orders his crew to heat cannonballs in
a fire until they are red-hot. When they
hit the *Congress*, the wooden ship bursts
into flame. Before the sailors abandon
ship, though, one of them fires a gun
at Captain Buchanan and hits him in

the leg. As Captain Buchanan is carried belowdecks, Lieutenant Jones takes over, but the battle is nearly finished. With one Northern ship at the bottom of the sea and another burning on the shore, the South has easily won.

Then, another Northern ship, the *Minnesota*, arrives. The *Virginia* fires, but is too far away to hit it. Shallow water keeps the *Virginia* from moving closer, so

Lt. Jones orders the *Virginia* back to port as darkness falls on Hampton Roads.

All night, the *Cumberland* burns, lighting the sky. The battle was a terrible blow for the Northern navy. The South's ironclad is more dangerous than anyone expected. There is only one hope for the sailors at Hampton Roads—the *Monitor.*

Luckily, the *Monitor* soon arrives to protect the *Minnesota.* The crew is tired from the long, dangerous trip. They have not slept for days. Captain Worden talks to his crew. He knows they are scared and worried. He tells them that he is proud of them and that they will fight well tomorrow. Even so, few men sleep that night.

The two ironclads are set to battle. Which one will win?

The next morning, a tower of black
smoke appears on the Elizabeth River. It
is the *Virginia*, heading straight for the
Minnesota! At 8:30 a.m. on March 9, 1862,
the battle begins.

No one knows who fires the first shot.
Most believe that the *Virginia* fires first on
the *Minnesota*. Though the *Minnesota* is hit
and slightly damaged, it fires back. But its
cannonballs do little harm to the *Virginia*.
It looks like the *Minnesota* is doomed. But
the *Monitor* joins the battle just in time,

and Captain Worden pilots the ship in front of the *Minnesota* to protect it. The two ironclads fire cannonballs back and forth. But neither ship is seriously damaged.

On shore, over 20,000 people gather to watch the battle—including hundreds of soldiers. The Northern army fires on the *Virginia*, but the bullets do not stop the ship. The cannons roar like thunder.

Smoke fills the harbor. The battle rages on and on. Heavy cannonballs that would have destroyed any wooden ship in the world only dent the ironclads.

In the *Monitor's* pilothouse, Captain Worden watches the battle and shouts orders to his crew. He peers out the pilothouse's narrow window, trying to get a better view of the *Virginia.*

SMASH!

A cannonball hits the pilothouse, right where Captain Worden stands! Miraculously, he survives, but splinters of metal pierce his eyeballs and blind him. Below deck, the ship doctor tries to remove the splinters. Captain Worden will later regain his sight, but he cannot lead the *Monitor* now. Lieutenant Greene takes command and steers the *Monitor* away. The crew needs time to recover from the blow.

Meanwhile, the *Virginia* tries to attack the *Minnesota*. But it cannot get close enough to fire because the water is too shallow. The two ironclads have been fighting for over three hours with no end in sight.

Suddenly, the *Virginia* springs a leak from one of the many hits it has taken. The ship retreats to the Elizabeth River. The *Monitor's* crew cheers. The battle is finally over!

But who won?

Both sides claim victory. The *Virginia* hurt the blockade. And it is clearly a serious threat to the North. But the *Monitor* protected the *Minnesota*. It stopped the *Virginia's* terrible attack. The blockade is still strong. And the North still has control of Hampton Roads.

After the battle, one reporter wrote, "iron will be the king of the seas." He was right. The clash forever changed how ships fight at sea. Countries stopped building wooden ships and built this new type of ship, called monitors. Only five days after the battle, the Northern navy ordered six more ironclads to be built. The powerful design of the little *Monitor* led to the huge battleships of today.

Chapter 4

What happened to the *Monitor* and the *Virginia* after their fierce battle? The two ships never fought again. In May 1862, the Northern army captured Norfolk, Virginia, where the *Virginia* was stationed. The crew of the *Virginia* did not want the North to have their prize ship. So they blew it up before they fled the city.

Meanwhile, the *Monitor* steamed up and down the coast, firing at Southern forts. It never went to battle again. Like the South, the North did not want its powerful ironclad to fall into enemy hands.

But on Christmas Day, 1862, the *Monitor* was ordered to go to Beaufort, North Carolina. The ship would become part of the Northern blockade there. The new captain, John Bankhead, and his crew were worried about the trip. The North Carolina coast was often stormy. The sailors remembered how the *Monitor* had almost sunk during a storm on its first voyage. The crew decided to have the *Monitor* towed by a big, powerful steamer called the *Rhode Island*—just in case a storm hit.

The two ships sailed out on December 29, 1862. The sky was clear and the sea was calm. But the next day, the wind picked up. Captain Bankhead was concerned. He sent a message to the *Rhode Island* that if the *Monitor* needed help, he would hang a red lantern.

That night, rough seas tossed the *Monitor.* Gigantic waves knocked the crew

off their feet. And to make matters worse,
all the lifeboats had been moved to the
Rhode Island. If the *Monitor's* crew needed
to abandon ship, they would have to wait
to be rescued by the *Rhode Island.*

On the *Monitor,* the sailors tried
desperately to save the ship. They bailed
water, but it came in faster than they
could get it out. Soon, there was over
a foot of water in the ironclad! As the
Monitor struggled in the raging seas,
it put the *Rhode Island* at risk. Captain

Bankhead knew that the *Monitor* could sink and take the *Rhode Island* with it. So he ordered the towrope to be cut. The two sailors who went to cut the rope were washed overboard. They disappeared into the black, swirling sea—and drowned.

Finally, Captain Bankhead gave up on saving the ship. A sailor hung a red lantern from the gun turret of the *Monitor*.

Rescue boats set off from the *Rhode Island*, bobbing like apples in the raging

sea. The sailors were terrified—but they
were determined to save the *Monitor's* crew.

When the lifeboats from the *Rhode Island*
arrived, Captain Bankhead ordered the
crew off the *Monitor.* The water in the
ironclad was now waist-deep. Most crew
members scrambled into rowboats. But
some men clung to the turret. The small
rowboats were so full that they seemed in
danger of sinking, too! Captain Bankhead
told the men to get into the rowboats, but

they refused. They felt it was safer to wait for another round of rescue boats.

This decision would cost them their lives.

Waves tossed the tiny rowboats as the men clung to the sides. At last, they made it to the *Rhode Island*. A huge wave smashed one of the lifeboats just as the *Rhode Island's* crew dragged the men aboard. Another rowboat was sent back to the *Monitor* for the sailors who still clung to the gun turret. It was almost there when, suddenly, the *Monitor,* the red lantern, and the men disappeared into the dark waters. That night, 16 men drowned, lost with the ironclad beneath the ocean waves.

Chapter 5

The *Monitor* was gone, but not forgotten. As the years passed, people kept searching for the ship. Yet without knowing exactly where the *Monitor* had sunk, it seemed impossible to find.

In 1973, two people started searching for the *Monitor* in a different way. Gordon Watts and Dorothy Nicholson knew the *Rhode Island* had towed the ironclad. By reading the *Rhode Island's* record book and re-creating the ship's route, they believed they could find the *Monitor*.

Watts and Nicholson studied maps and charts of the Atlantic Ocean. These documents gave them more clues about where the *Monitor* had sunk. They made

their own maps and charts. Finally, they concluded that the *Monitor* must have sunk in Hatteras, off the coast of North Carolina.

In August 1973, a group of scientists set out for Hatteras on a ship called the *Eastward*. They used the map that Watts and Nicholson had created. Like a treasure map, *X* marked the spot where they hoped to find the *Monitor*.

The scientists brought along a lot of equipment. Underwater cameras, sonar devices, and television monitors would help them find the ship, but it would not be easy. They had to search 96 square miles of ocean floor and the hundreds of shipwrecks that lay in the "Graveyard of the Atlantic."

By the end of the first week, the scientists had found 21 possible ships.

One of the most important tools they used was sonar. Sonar sends sound waves through the ocean. The sound waves bounce off objects on the ocean floor and make patterns on a screen. Scientists can tell the size of the objects from the patterns. Most of the 21 objects at Hatteras were the wrong size. But one was the right size—and the right shape.

Had they finally found the *Monitor?*

No, it was just part of another ship.

As the days passed, the scientists began to lose hope. Would they ever find the *Monitor?* Then, a funny accident gave them an important clue. One of the scientists, Fred Kelly, decided to go fishing. He used the sonar to look for fish in the ocean. To his surprise, the sonar

found something more than fish—
something that looked like it might be
the *Monitor*. He showed it to the other
scientists. What was it? They took a
closer look.

The scientists sent down a sensitive
underwater camera. It showed the
outline of a shipwreck. Even more
amazing was what seemed to be the
famous gun turret resting upside down
on the deck. The shapes of the ship and
the turret matched the *Monitor* exactly!
The scientists cheered. They were sure
that they had solved the mystery of
where the *Monitor* had sunk!

In 1974, a research ship, the *Alcoa
Seaprobe,* went back to the site of the
shipwreck to take more photos. Like
pieces of a giant puzzle, scientists put

the photos together until they had a complete picture of the *Monitor*. More questions arose with the photographs. For instance, why was the *Monitor* broken into two pieces? Scientists believe that when the ship hit the ocean floor, the gun turret fell onto the deck.

After so many years in the ocean, the *Monitor* was in bad shape. Decay caused by seawater had made the ship's strong iron as fragile as glass. The ship could fall apart if it was moved. Since the *Monitor* could not be safely brought to the surface, it had to be protected where it was. In 1975, scientists convinced Congress to make the shipwreck a marine sanctuary. That meant that no one could explore or disturb the *Monitor* without permission.

But as time passed, scientists realized that the harsh conditions in the ocean could completely destroy the *Monitor*. Bit by bit, divers brought parts of the ironclad, including its engine and anchor, to the surface. But the real challenge would be raising the gun turret. Could they do it?

Chapter 6

John Broadwater, director of the Monitor National Marine Sanctuary, knew that the *Monitor's* gun turret was like a sunken treasure. He wanted to bring that treasure to the surface before it was destroyed and lost forever. Working with Commander Bobbie Scholley of the Navy's Mobile Diving and Salvage Unit, he came up with a plan.

A team of over 150 divers and scientists worked together to raise the gun turret. A huge barge floated near the sunken ship. Divers attached a giant, eight-legged claw called a "spider" to the gun turret. They began to slowly lift it to the surface. Finally, on August 9,

2002, the gun turret broke through the surface. It was placed on the waiting barge. A parade of ships brought the turret to The Mariners' Museum in Newport News, Virginia, where a 21-gun salute greeted its arrival. Hundreds of people came to watch the *Monitor's* gun turret return to Virginia.

After being in the ocean for so long, the gun turret was full of mud. Workers used a pump to remove it. The inside of the turret was cold and damp. Even after

spending years underwater, it still smelled like coal! Scientists say it will take about 10 years to fully clean the gun turret. It will then be coated with a special liquid to protect it from moisture. Like detectives, the workers sift carefully through the silt, searching for artifacts. So far, they have found buttons, coins, pocketknives, and a wool coat. They also found a wedding ring and a silver piece with initials carved on it. All of these items help paint a picture of what life was like on the ship.

The most important finds inside the gun turret were two human bones, which were sent to a laboratory in Hawaii. There, scientists will study them and try to identify them. Then the bones will be returned to the relatives of the lost crew for a burial ceremony.

Every day, scientists learn more about life on the *Monitor.* Even though they are not finished excavating the gun turret, it is on display at The Mariners' Museum— not far from where the *Monitor* fought the *Virginia.* Today, everyone can see this important part of the *Monitor*—the amazing ironclad that changed the world!